LEADER GUIDE

ORDINARY PEOPLE CAN DO THE EXTRAORDINARY

Biblical Success Models for the African American Community

Colleen Birchett, Ph.D.
Editor

A UMI Publication
urban ministries, inc.
Chicago, IL 60643

Publisher
Urban Ministries, Inc.
1350 West 103rd Street
Chicago, Illinois 60643
(312) 233-4499

First Edition
First Printing
ISBN: 0-940955-23-7
Catalog No. 3-2410

Copyright © 1993 by Urban Ministries, Inc. All rights reserved. No part of this publication may be reproduced, stored in a retrieval system, or transmitted in any form or by any means, electronic, mechanical, photocopy, recording or otherwise except for brief quotations in printed reviews without prior written permission from the holder of the copyright.

Scripture quotations are from the King James Version of the Bible unless otherwise stated. Printed in the United States of America.

DEDICATION

To the thousands of people who lead Bible studies in churches throughout the world.

CONTENTS

ACKNOWLEDGMENTS 5
PREFACE   *Dr. Colleen Birchett*   7
INTRODUCTION   *Dr. Colleen Birchett*   9

I.   Micah: Brother, Where Are Your Clothes?
                              Dr. John Little   15

II.   Hosea: What's Love Got to Do With It?
                              Prof. Marvin Goodwin   19

III.   Amos: Fruit Mixed With Poetry
                              Chaplain Andrew Calhoun   23

IV.   Abraham: From the Ghetto to Greatness
                              Rabbi Sanford H. Shudnow   27

V.   Moses: Let My People Go!
                              Rabbi Sanford H. Shudnow   31

VI.   Deborah: Sister, Take Charge!
                              Chaplain Melody Goodwin   37

VII.   Samuel: The Man in the Middle
                              Minister Mark Jeffers   41

VIII. David: A Boy from the 'Hood
                              Chaplain Melody Goodwin   45

IX.   Solomon: Lord, Give Me Common Sense
                              Jenifer Campbell   49

X.   Elijah: Strange But Powerful
                              Dr. Kenneth Hammonds   53

XI.   Josiah: It's Not Where You Come From
                              Dr. Bennie Goodwin   57

XII.   Jeremiah: Hope in Spite of Tears
                              Dr. Kenneth Hammonds   61

ACKNOWLEDGMENTS

We wish to acknowledge the outstanding contributions of publications manager and designer, Shawan Brand; copy editor, Mary C. Lewis; and publications assistant, Carolyn Cummings, Caron B. Davis, and Cheryl Wilson, without whose help the book could not have come into existence. Last, but not least, we wish to thank Media Graphics Corporation and Dickinson Press, Inc.

PREFACE

Dr. Colleen Birchett

The Old Testament is filled with interesting biographies. In these life stories, one can read about the ways in which God became very personal to individuals in very personal situations. From these stories, one can draw parallels and spiritual principles which can be applied in the 20th century, for every phase of the human life cycle.

Ordinary People Can Do the Extraordinary presents an overview of 12 biblical biographies. Each chapter provides an overview of a given biblical character's life, and includes questions to help the reader abstract principles from the person's life and apply them to life among African Americans today. The characters are found in a variety of political, economic and spiritual circumstances. One common thread is that these great men and women of God loved the Lord because He heard their cry.

Objectives. Upon completion of this book, the reader should be able to discuss the lives of 12 biblical characters, discuss spiritual principles which their lives teach, and explain ways in which these principles apply to life among African Americans in the 20th century. A goal of the book is to stimulate more in-depth Bible study into the lives of the characters featured in the book, and the lives of other characters of the Old and New Testaments.

Uses. The book and its Leader's Guide can be used for private as well as group study, in a variety of ways in the local church: a) training of teachers and deacons; b) Sunday School electives; c) Training Hour curriculum; d) weekday Bible studies; e) Vacation Bible School curriculum for the adult class; f) family devotions.

Group Study - 90 Minute Sessions. The book is designed for a two-part group study session. Part I would allow participants to study the exposition of a Bible character's life, and to discuss, together, the Scripture passage and review activity at the end of each chapter. A session leader would divide the group into smaller groups and allow them, during Part II, to discuss the topics under "The African American Connection."

The small group discussions provide every participant the opportunity to contribute to the group's understanding and application of the material being presented. A different topic from "The African American Connection" section would be assigned to each small group. Then they should reconvene with the larger group and report their findings. For the chapters which have this section, allow for discussion of "What Do You Think?" questions.

Group Study - 60 Minute Sessions. In shorter periods, it might be necessary to use part of a given chapter as a stimulus for discussion during the group meeting itself. Then the rest of the chapter might be used as a "homework" assignment or for private devotional study.

Family Devotions. During the week preceding the study of a given chapter, all members would read a given chapter privately. However, each family member would be assigned a different question from among "The African American Connection" questions. When it is time to have devotions, each family member would provide an overview of a chapter. Then, "round robin" style, each member would read his/her assigned question and present his/her opinion concerning "The African American Connection."

The Leader Guide. This leader guide is designed to assist leaders of large and small group discussions related to the book, *Ordinary People Can Do the Extraordinary*. The guide contains an introductory chapter on leading group discussions. It also contains lesson plans—one for exploring each chapter. Each lesson plan is in two parts. Part I focuses on the biblical character and in Part II, participants form small groups to explore "The African American Connection."

Summary. The book can be used in a variety of ways. However, the main objective is that Christians learn important spiritual truths from the lives of great men and women of God, and apply those truths to their lives in the 20th century.

TALK SHOW HOSTS:
Models For Leading Discussions

Dr. Colleen Birchett

So you have been asked to guide group discussions related to the book, *Ordinary People Can Do the Extraordinary*. Chances are, if you are like most people facing such a challenge, you are wondering how to prepare. By reading this leader guide, you are taking the first step. However, in all likelihood, you may still be uncertain about how you can make this upcoming experience most rewarding for the participants.

You may be wondering where, outside of reading this book, you might get help in preparing yourself. Well, help may be no farther away than your television set. Why not observe the many television talk show hosts (on Christian and other stations) who meet challenges similar to yours every day? Notice some of their techniques. Then prepare to use those that you find effective as you guide your participants through the contents of *Ordinary People Can Do the Extraordinary*.

While people vary in their opinions about Phil Donahue, in "Phil Donahue: An Excellent Model for Leading a Discussion," Jeff Passe says that Phil is one of the best discussion leaders. Passe identifies several techniques which can be studied and practiced in leading group discussions. They are useful in church settings as well. A discussion leader can:

    a) Study the material to be discussed beforehand;
    b) Present a background on the topic before the discussion;
    c) Take steps to relax the participants;
    d) Avoid embarrassing people;
    e) Keep the discussion moving;
    f) Reword statements that participants may not understand;
    g) Prevent anyone from monopolizing the discussion or straying from the topic;

    h) Encourage the expression of feelings, while avoiding intellectualizing;
    i) Use humor to reduce tension;
    j) Ask good questions.

Preparing Beforehand. Whether your favorite talk show host is Phil Donahue, Oprah Winfrey, Ted Koppel, Rev. Pat Robertson, or Rev. Jesse Jackson, one thing is certain, all of these hosts are familiar with their subject matter before they open their discussions. Therefore, most of them do not waste time asking boring or irrevelant questions.

Leaders who guide discussions related to *Ordinary People Can Do the Extraordinary* can prepare by reading, beforehand, the chapter to be discussed. Spend time reviewing and developing thoughts concerning, "The African American Connection" section. This section will be the subject of small and large group discussions. Having studied the chapter, it will be much easier to guide the discussions.

Presenting Background Information. The openings of television talk shows are intriguing. Rev. Pat Robertson and Ted Koppel are masters of this technique. Their video vignettes are almost scientifically designed to arrest viewers' attention and direct them to the most important aspects of the issues being explored. The openings' specific formats vary based on the topic. An intriguing question, a statement from a participant, the relaying of a personal testimony, or the reading of some startling facts or statistics—are all used to attract our attention.

In group sessions on *Ordinary People Can Do the Extraordinary,"* the substance for such creative openings can be gathered from the chapters themselves.

Relaxing the Group. Oprah Winfrey's audiences always seem relaxed and engaged in the program. When individuals respond on the air, they usually seem poised and/or ready to "bare their souls" to Oprah, the viewing audience and her guests. Both Oprah and Phil facilitate this by "warming up" to their audiences. They may place their arm around a respondent's shoulders, they may laugh or even cry with the participant—

whatever is necessary to build trust. Both Phil and Oprah are very supportive of their studio audience.

Talk show hosts take the steps necessary to build an environment that is safe for the expression of differing viewpoints. One important means for you to achieve this with your participants is to arrange the room in a circle or similar shape so that participants can view one another and interact more easily. One rule that may be abandoned is having everyone stand and face the class. By arranging the chairs so that they are already facing one another, interaction is achieved more naturally.

Avoiding Embarrassment. Regardless of the topic, there is always the possibility that someone will make a statement that is unpopular, unreasonable, or a "slip." In other instances, someone may make statements designed to rile the audience, stage a protest, or upset the proceedings. Notice how talk show hosts avoid this problem by controlling the microphone, redirecting the discussion, affirming the response whenever possible or quickly changing the subject.

Most talk show hosts are aware of the hazards of "mob psychology" and the potential for seriously damaging a participant's self-esteem. The discussion leader's responsibility is to protect individuals with unusual viewpoints as much as this is possible. This is especially important in an environment where it is hoped that people will come to a saving knowledge of our Lord Jesus Christ. This can happen when a person feels loved and nurtured. It is in this type of environment that people are most likely to be open to the truth. One is not open to the truth if one is embarrassed, so be mindful of your role as leader—to nurture participants' sense of worth while being ready to redirect discussion if someone tries to jeopardize anyone's self-esteem.

Keeping the Discussion Moving. Talk shows rarely become dull. That is because the hosts have mastered the science of keeping the discussion moving. Several methods exist of achieving this. One way is to use interesting angles for each topic. To do this, examine the lives of the various biblical characters, consider "The African American Connection" and think of a creative way to make this connection interesting for the group with which you are dealing.

Sufficient planning is required in order to keep the discussion moving. One must be able to anticipate the points where discussion may likely lag, and then have at one's disposal, ways of moving it along. Bringing magazine and newspaper articles (local and national), slides, overhead transparencies or photographs, using them to illustrate certain points, and encouraging reactions are all ways of keeping the discussion moving.

Rewording Statements. Ted Koppel, host of "Night Line" is a master of rewording statements. Frequently his guests talk in the jargon of their professions, or they take a lot of time to state indirectly what their real opinions are. Koppel often follows their statements by rewording them, based on his understanding. By doing this, he also clarifies comments for the audience.

Often he prefaces his rewording with, "Correct me if I am wrong, but what I hear you to be saying..., Is your point...," or "Then, what's your point?" This technique is useful for clarifying a participant's statement for the larger group, for nurturing insecure participants, and for encouraging them to take more risks in the group.

Avoiding Tangents and Controlling Monopolizers. Among the special guests and participants of any talk show are those who like to dominate a discussion or take it on various tangents. This also happens in church meetings. Therefore, in order to prevent boredom and encourage the participants' regular attendance, a workshop leader must control the amount of input that monopolizers and tangent takers are allowed to have.

Notice how Phil Donahue does this by controlling the microphone. When it becomes obvious that a speaker is monopolizing or is taking the group on a tangent, Phil moves to the next speaker. He also controls it by his selection of speakers from the audience. In some way, discussion leaders can use their power to call on participants, and a well-structured discussion can result.

Encouraging the Expression of Feelings. Oprah is masterful at this. She very carefully controls the amount of "intellectualizing," and instead focuses on people's feelings and reactions to various realities. Her "experts" are encouraged to talk in a down to earth manner so that the viewing and studio audiences can understand her or him.

This is very important, in the environment of the church, where it is hoped that healing and nurturance can take place and people will feel loved. Encourage participants to express their feelings, and then reword statements so that each person knows s/he is understood.

Using Humor. Both Phil and Oprah use humor to reduce tensions. Often, at a moment of great intensity, they will insert a mild joke, in order to evoke a friendly laugh from the audience. Usually this has the effect of reducing tension. Silly comments, "off the cuff" remarks and exaggerations, can also serve this purpose.

Humor can help to remove a climate of uneasy feelings. Discomfort such as this could lower attendance and stifle participation. Therefore, it is important to use humor and other techniques to create a sense of warmth and ease.

Asking Good Questions. Rev. Jesse Jackson and Ted Koppel are masters of the art of asking good questions. Rarely does one find them asking closed–ended questions which require merely a "yes" or "no" response. Their questions are consistent with well-defined objectives, designed to take the discussion where they want it to go. These are techniques that Bible discussion leaders can employ to get at deeper truths of Scripture. However, using this technique effectively requires preparation and planning.

Conclusions and Summaries. Most talk show hosts, due to the constraints of time, are unable to review and summarize properly. However, in a church setting, where there are fewer constraints of time, it may be possible to prepare a summary and present it at the end of each discussion session.

Adapting Content for Specific Needs. Talk show hosts on television cannot tailor their content so that it meets the needs of all segments of the viewer audience. However, discussion leaders in local churches may be able to do this for their particular congregation. *Ordinary People Can Do the Extraordinary* has general content for a general church audience. As a discussion leader in your particular church, familiar with your particular participants, you may be able to develop examples and applications that refer to specific lives, interests and concerns. This is one way of keeping the discussion moving and making it more relevant.

Preparing Participants for the Discussion. After the first meeting of class, encourage the students to read the material for the next session beforehand. Different participants can be assigned to answer different questions from "The African American Connection" section. In this way, the participants can be well-informed when they approach the discussion, and this may have an impact on the richness of the ideas exchanged. This is an advantage that discussion leaders in small churches have over talk show hosts.

Summary. This article has suggested just a few of several techniques for making your discussion of the book, *Ordinary People Can Do the Extraordinary* come alive. These techniques are employed by several popular talk show hosts, and you can adapt them for the church setting. However, it is important to keep in mind that the most effective discussion leader of all time is our Lord Jesus Christ Himself. By studying His manner of dealing with the woman at the well, Nicodemus, Peter and others, one can see many of the techniques mentioned here. The most important goal of all is to foster a climate in which people can come to a saving knowledge of Jesus Christ and improve their relationships with Him.

Bibliography

Kozma, Robert B., Lawrence W. Belle and George W. Williams. *Instructional Techniques in Higher Education*. Englewood Cliffs, New Jersey: Educational Technology Publications, 1978.

Maier, N.R.F. *Problem-Solving Discussions and Conferences*. New York: McGraw-Hill, 1963.

Passe, Jeff. "Phil Donahue: An Excellent Model for Leading a Discussion." *Journal of Teacher Education,* Volume XXXV, No. 1, January, 1984, pp. 43-48.

CHAPTER ONE

MICAH:
Brother, Where Are Your Clothes?

Format for Sessions of 90 Minutes or More

PART ONE		PART TWO	
TIME	ACTIVITY	TIME	ACTIVITY
5 min.	Prayer	25 min.	Small Group Study
5 min.	Scripture	20 min.	Large Group Presentations
15 min.	Scripture Search	5 min.	Prayer
15 min.	Chapter Highlights		

For sessions of less than 90 minutes, use PART ONE only, and assign the case study as homework

LESSON AIMS: At the end of this two–part session, the participant should be able to: a) provide an overview of the life of Micah the prophet; b) discuss the historical context in which Micah lived; c) discuss the message Micah brought to the people; d) apply principles from the life of Micah to African Americans today.

ORDINARY PEOPLE CAN DO THE EXTRAORDINARY

I. PART ONE

A. PRAYER

Open the session with prayer, including the lesson aims.

B. SCRIPTURE

1. Summarize and review Micah 1:1-4; 4:1-5; 6:6-8; and 7:18-19.
2. Direct students to the "Scripture Search" section near the end of the chapter.
3. Ask students to circle the correct answer for each question.
4. After about ten minutes ask for volunteers to answer the questions.
5. Answers: 1. b; 2. b; 3. a; 4. c; 5. e.

C. CHAPTER HIGHLIGHTS

Explain that the chapter focuses on Micah. Using Chapter One as background, provide a general overview of the chapter. You may want to use "Let's Discover" as a starting point. Be sure to include the following topics:

1. Micah's Time
2. Micah's Method
3. Micah's Message

II. PART TWO

A. THE AFRICAN AMERICAN CONNECTION

1. Introduction

    The "African American Connection" section provides the opportunity to apply principles from Micah's life to African American lives today.

2. Procedure

Select Small Group Leaders. Ask for volunteers or select three small group leaders. Then assign each small group leader a number, 1–3. This can also be done beforehand to facilitate a smoother meeting time. Ask the small group leaders to write their numbers on large sheets of white paper so that they can be seen from a distance.

Divide into Small Groups. Inform the participants that they will be broken down into three small groups. Each group will study various questions related to principles from Micah's life, and will present their findings to the larger group at the end of the small group study period. The questions to be studied should correspond to the number of groups as follows:

Group #1: Communicate Clearly
Group #2: Lead Unofficially
Group #3: Take Risks

Allow the Participants to Count Off by Threes. Then ask them to follow the small group leader holding their respective assigned numbers. Inform them of the location where each of the groups will be meeting. These locations can also be printed, beforehand, on a sheet of paper, copied and distributed, so as to facilitate a smoother meeting time.

Participants should follow small group leaders that display their numbers to respective meeting areas. Allow participants to assemble into smaller groups.

B. SMALL GROUP STUDY

1. Small Group Leaders

For each topic, there are several related questions to stimulate discussion. Each small group will have one topic to explore.

2. Sharing Insights

After ten minutes, designate someone who will summarize the small group discussion within the larger body of participants. Remind the designated person that she/he will only have one minute to present.

C. LARGE GROUP PRESENTATIONS

1. Large Group Leader

Reconvene the Group. Call the small groups back together.

Explain the Procedure. Explain that a representative of each small group will share that group's reflections on the African American connection with the larger group.

Remind Small Group Representatives of the Time. Remind each small group representative that she/he should try to summarize his/her group's discussion in one minute.

It may be necessary to pose questions that require them to relate their small group presentations to the Bible and to generalize it to modern times.

Assignment. Assign participants to read Chapter Two, about Hosea, in preparation for the next session. Encourage them to read all or parts of the two books recommended at the end of the chapter.

D. PRAYER

Hold hands, form a circle, and ask for specific prayer requests. Then ask for several volunteers to pray, keeping the prayer requests in mind.

CHAPTER TWO

HOSEA:
What's Love Got to Do With It?

Format for Sessions of 90 Minutes or More

PART ONE		PART TWO	
TIME	ACTIVITY	TIME	ACTIVITY
5 min.	Prayer	25 min.	Small Group Study
5 min.	Scripture	20 min.	Large Group Presentations
15 min.	Scripture Search	5 min.	Prayer
15 min.	Chapter Highlights		

For sessions of less than 90 minutes, use PART ONE only, and assign the case study as homework

LESSON AIMS: At the end of this two–part session, the participant should be able to: a) present an overview of Hosea's life; b) discuss the historical context in which Hosea lived; c) explain Hosea's message from God; d) apply principles from Hosea's life to lives of African Americans today.

ORDINARY PEOPLE CAN DO THE EXTRAORDINARY

I. PART ONE

A. PRAYER

Open the session with prayer, including the lesson aims.

B. SCRIPTURE

1. Summarize and review Hosea 1:1-4, 6-9; 3:1-5; 6:1-3.
2. Direct students to the "Scripture Search" section near the end of the chapter.
3. Ask students to match the numbers in the first column with the corresponding letters in the second column.
4. After about ten minutes, ask for volunteers to present their answers.
5. Answers: 1. E; 2. C; 3. D; 4. A; 5. B.

C. CHAPTER HIGHLIGHTS

Explain that the chapter focuses on Hosea and ask a volunteer to read aloud the "Let's Discover" section to stimulate interest. Use Chapter Two as background, and provide a general overview of the points made in the chapter. Be sure to include:

1. Hosea the Man
2. Hosea's Wife
3. Hosea's Call
4. Hosea's Times
5. Hosea's Message (Chapters 4—14)

II. PART TWO

A. THE AFRICAN AMERICAN CONNECTION

1. Introduction

   The section provides the opportunity to apply principles from Hosea's life to African American lives today.

2. Procedure

Select Small Group Leaders. Ask for volunteers or select two group leaders. Then assign each small group leader a number, 1–2. If you prefer to have participants form more than two groups, assign numbers accordingly (so that four or six groups form). This can be done beforehand to facilitate a smoother meeting time. Ask the small group leaders to write the numbers on large sheets of paper so that they can be seen from a distance.

Divide into Small Groups. Inform the participants that they will broken down into two (or more) groups. Each group will study a different question involving applying principles from Hosea's life as it applies to life among African Americans today as follows:

Group #1 The Family
Group #2 The Church

If more than two groups form, participants can still discuss the two topics. Each group will probably emerge with their own insights to share.

Allow the Participants to Count Off by Twos (or More). Then ask them to follow the small group leader holding their respective assigned numbers. Inform them of the location of the room (or building) where each of the groups will be meeting. These locations can be printed, beforehand, on a sheet of paper, copied and distributed.

Ask the small group leaders to display their numbers so that people having that number can follow them to their respective meeting places. Then allow the participants to assemble into the smaller groups.

B. SMALL GROUP STUDY

1. Small Group Leaders

   Each small group will have one topic to discuss.

2. Sharing Insights

   After ten minutes, designate someone to summarize the small group discussion within the larger body. Remind designated person that s/he will only have one minute.

C. LARGE GROUP PRESENTATIONS

1. Large Group Leader

   Reconvene the Group. Call the small groups back together.

   Explain the Procedure. Explain that a representative of each small group will share that group's reflections on applications from the life of Hosea. Participants should relate "What Do You Think?" questions to the topics discussed. Encourage those who have read the "Books Recommended" to share any insights gained.

   Remind Small Group Representatives of the Time. Remind each small group representative that s/he should try to summarize his/her group's discussion in one minute.

   Assignment. Assign Chapter Three, about the Book of Amos, for participants to read between sessions in preparation for the discussion on Chapter Three.

D. PRAYER

Hold hands, form a circle, and ask for specific prayer requests. Then ask for several volunteers to pray, keeping the prayer requests in mind.

CHAPTER THREE

AMOS:
Fruit Mixed With Poetry

Format for Sessions of 90 Minutes or More

PART ONE		PART TWO	
TIME	ACTIVITY	TIME	ACTIVITY
5 min.	Prayer	25 min.	Small Group Study
5 min.	Scripture	20 min.	Large Group Presentations
15 min.	Scripture Search	5 min.	Prayer
15 min.	Chapter Highlights		

For sessions of less than 90 minutes, use PART ONE only, and assign the case study as homework

LESSON AIMS: At the end of this two–part session, the participant should be able to: a) present a general overview of the life of Amos, the prophet; b) summarize Amos's message from God for the people; c) discuss the historical context in which Amos carried out his ministry; d) discuss Amos's leadership qualities; e) apply principles from Amos's life to lives of today's African Americans.

ORDINARY PEOPLE CAN DO THE EXTRAORDINARY

I. PART ONE

A. PRAYER

Open the session with prayer, including the lesson aims.

B. SCRIPTURE

1. Summarize and review Amos 1:1-2; 3:1-8; 7:14-15; 9:13-15.
2. Direct students to the "Scripture Search" section of the chapter, instructing them to fill in the blanks.
3. Allow students to work independently for about ten minutes.
4. After about ten minutes ask for volunteers to share their answers.
5. Answers: 1. farmer; 2. worship; 3. loyal; 4. hope; 5. water, stream.

C. CHAPTER HIGHLIGHTS

Explain that the chapter focuses on Amos. Use Chapter Three as background, and provide a general overview of the points made in the chapter. Be sure to include the following topics:

1. Amos's Calling and Commission
2. Amos's Context for Ministry
3. Amos's Message to Israel
4. Amos's Leadership Qualities

II. PART TWO

A. THE AFRICAN AMERICAN CONNECTION

1. Introduction

   The "African American Connection" section provides the

opportunity to apply principles from Amos's life to African American lives today.

2. Procedure

Select Small Group Leaders. Ask for volunteers or select four small group leaders. Then assign each small group leader a number, 1–4. (This can be done beforehand.) Ask the small group leaders to write their numbers on large sheets of white paper so that they can be seen from a distance.

Divide into Small Groups. Inform the group of participants that they will be divided into four small groups. Each group will study various questions related to the life of Amos and will present their findings to the larger group at the end of the small group study period. The questions to be studied should correspond to the number of the group as follows:

Group #1 Economics
Group #2 Education
Group #3 Politics
Group #4 Anti-Social Behavior

Allow the Participants to Count Off by Fours. Then ask them to follow the small group leader holding their respective assigned numbers. Inform them of the location of the room (or building) where each of the groups (1–4) will be meeting. These locations can be printed, beforehand, on a sheet of paper, copied and distributed.

Ask the small group leaders to display their numbers so that persons having that number can follow them to their respective meeting places. Then allow the participants to assemble into the smaller groups.

B. SMALL GROUP STUDY

1. Small Group Leaders

   For each topic, there are several related questions to stimulate discussion. Therefore, each small group will have one topic to explore.

2. Sharing Insights

   After ten minutes, designate someone to summarize the small group discussion within the larger body of training session participants. Remind the designated person that she/he will only have one minute to present.

C. LARGE GROUP PRESENTATIONS

1. Large Group Leader

   Reconvene the Group. Call the small groups back together.

   Explain the Procedure. Explain that a representative of each small group will share that group's reflections on applications from Amos's life.

   Remind Small Group Representatives of the Time. Remind each small group representative that she/he should try to summarize his/her group's discussion in one minute.

   Assignment. Assign participants to read Chapter Four, about Abraham, in preparation for the next session.

D. PRAYER

Hold hands, form a circle, and ask for specific prayer requests. Then ask for several volunteers to pray, keeping the prayer requests in mind.

CHAPTER FOUR

ABRAHAM:
From the Ghetto to Greatness

Format for Sessions of 90 Minutes or More

PART ONE		PART TWO	
TIME	ACTIVITY	TIME	ACTIVITY
5 min.	Prayer	25 min.	Small Group Study
5 min.	Scripture	20 min.	Large Group Presentations
15 min.	Scripture Search	5 min.	Prayer
15 min.	Chapter Highlights		

For sessions of less than 90 minutes, use PART ONE only, and assign the case study as homework

LESSON AIMS: At the end of this two–part session, the participant should be able to: a) present basic facts about Abraham's background and personality; b) discuss Abraham's relationship with his family; c) present examples of Abraham's hospitality; d) discuss Abraham's relationship with God; e) identify principles from the life of Abraham that apply to African Americans today.

ORDINARY PEOPLE CAN DO THE EXTRAORDINARY

I. PART ONE

A. PRAYER

Open the session with prayer, including the lesson aims.

B. SCRIPTURE

1. Summarize Genesis 12:1–8; Hebrews 11:8-12
2. Direct participants' attention to the "Scripture Search" true and false statements in Chapter Four.
3. Allow about ten minutes for them to locate the related Scriptures and complete the "Scripture Search."
4. Answers: 1. T; 2. F; 3. F; 4. T; 5. T.

C. CHAPTER HIGHLIGHTS

Explain that the chapter focuses on Abraham. Using Chapter Four as background and "Let's Discover" as a starting point, provide a general overview of the points made in the chapter. Be sure to include the following topics:

1. What's in a Name?
2. Abraham's Birth and Background
3. Abraham as Husband
4. Abraham, Example of Hospitality
5. Abraham, Caring Family Member
6. Abraham, Lover of God, Father of God's People
7. Abraham's Self-Reliance
8. Abraham's Covenant with God

II. PART TWO

A. THE AFRICAN AMERICAN CONNECTION

1. Introduction

   Explain that the this section provides the opportunity to

make more applications of Abraham's personality and background to African Americans today.

2. Procedure

   Select Small Group Leaders. Ask for volunteers or select three small group leaders. Then assign each small group leader a number, 1–3. Ask the small group leaders to write their numbers on large sheets of white paper so that the numbers can be seen from a distance.

   Divide into Small Groups. Inform the participants that they will be broken into three small groups. Each group will study a different topic related to the Scripture passage, and will present its findings to the larger group at the end of the small group study period. The topics to be studied should correspond with the number of the group as follows:

   Group #1: Strong Role Models
   Group #2: Our Own Rhythm
   Group #3: Scars and Stars

   Allow the Participants to Count Off by Fours. Ask them to follow the small group leader holding their respective assigned numbers. Caution students to avoid joining the same group each time, but to try different groups. This can be achieved by beginning the numbering in a different section of the room than you did last week. Inform them of the location where each of the groups will be meeting. These locations can also be printed, beforehand, on a sheet of paper, copied and distributed, so as to facilitate a smoother meeting time.

   Ask the small group leaders to display their numbers so that persons having their number can follow them to their respective meeting places. Next allow participants to assemble into the smaller groups.

B. SMALL GROUP STUDY

1. Small Group Leaders

   There is one topic for each small group to discuss.

2. Sharing Insights

   After ten minutes, designate someone who will summarize the small group discussion within the larger body of training session participants. Remind the designated person that s/he will only have one minute to present.

C. LARGE GROUP PRESENTATIONS

1. Large Group Leader

   Reconvene the Group. Call the small groups back together.

   Explain the Procedure. Explain that a representative of each small group will share that group's reflections on applications from the life of Abraham with the larger group. Allow time for disscussion of "What Do You Think?" questions.

   Remind Small Group Representatives of the Time. Each small group representative should try to summarize his/her group's discussion in one minute. Be sure the small group presenters connect their small group presentations to the life of Abraham and that they draw parallels from his life to modern life.

   Assignment. Assign Chapter Five, to read by the next session.

D. PRAYER

Hold hands, form a circle, and ask for specific prayer requests. Then ask for several volunteers to pray, keeping the prayer requests in mind.

CHAPTER FIVE

MOSES:
Let My People Go!

Format for Sessions of 90 Minutes or More

PART ONE		PART TWO	
TIME	ACTIVITY	TIME	ACTIVITY
5 min.	Prayer	25 min.	Small Group Study
5 min.	Scripture	20 min.	Large Group Presentations
15 min.	Scripture Search	5 min.	Prayer
15 min.	Chapter Highlights		

For sessions of less than 90 minutes, use PART ONE only, and assign the case study as homework

LESSON AIMS: At the end of this two-part session the participant should be able to: a) present an overview of the birth and family background of Moses; b) explain how Moses built the nation of Israel; c) discuss Moses's humility; d) discuss leadership qualities of Moses; e) discuss Moses's relationship with God; f) apply principles from Moses's life to lives of African American today.

ORDINARY PEOPLE CAN DO THE EXTRAORDINARY

I. PART ONE

A. PRAYER

Open the session with prayer, including the lesson aims.

B. SCRIPTURE

1. Summarize and review Exodus 2:1-10; Hebrews 11:24-29.
2. Direct them to the "Scripture Search" section in the chapter.
3. Ask participants to fill in the blanks with the correct response.
4. After about ten minutes, ask for volunteers from each group to present their answers.
5. Answers: 1. Egypt; 2. water; 3. mother, daughter; 4. Jochebed, Zipporah, Aaron, Jethro; 5. humble, balance, prayer, God.

C. CHAPTER HIGHLIGHTS

Explain that the chapter focuses on Moses. Inform them that the chapter contains an overview of Moses's life and his contributions to the building of Israel. It also contains principles which can be applied to African Americans today. Using Chapter Five as background, summarize the points made in the chapter. Be sure to include the following topics:

1. Moses: The Man
2. Moses: Birth and Background
3. Moses: Nation Builder
4. Moses: God's Humble Servant
5. Moses: Man of Justice and Balance
6. Moses: Compassionate Shepherd
7. Moses: Man of Respect
8. Moses: The Team Leader
9. Moses: Learning How to Delegate

10. Moses: Man of Prayer
11. Moses: Servant of People
12. Moses: Man of God

II. PART TWO

A. THE AFRICAN AMERICAN CONNECTION

1. Introduction

   Explain that the "African American Connection" topics provide an opportunity to apply principles from Moses's life to African Americans today.

2. Procedure

   Select Small Group Leaders. Ask for volunteers or select two small group leaders. Then assign each small group leader a number, 1 or 2. This can be done beforehand to facilitate a smoother meeting time. You may prefer to have participants form more than two groups. In that case, more leaders will need to be designated for four or six groups. Ask the small group leaders to write their numbers on large sheets of white paper so that they can be seen from a distance.

   Divide into Small Groups. Inform the group of participants that they will form two (or more) small groups. Each group will discuss a different topic related to the chapter, and will present their findings to the larger group at the end of the small group study period. The topics of discussion should correspond with the number of the group as follows:

   Group #1: Conflicts
   Group #2: Dream Keepers

If you are forming more than two groups, each of the two topics can be explored by more than one group.

Allow the Participants to Count Off by Twos (or More). Then ask them to follow the small group leader holding their respective assigned numbers. Inform them of the location of the room (or building) where each of the groups will be meeting. These locations can be printed, beforehand, on a sheet of paper, copied and distributed, so as to facilitate a smoother meeting time.

Ask the small group leaders to display their numbers so that persons having their numbers can follow them to their respective meeting places. Then allow the participants to assemble into the smaller groups.

B. SMALL GROUP STUDY

1. Small Group Leaders

   For each topic, there are several related questions to stimulate discussion. Therefore, each small group will have one topic to complete.

2. Sharing Insights

   After ten minutes, small group leaders should designate someone to summarize the small group discussion for the larger body of session participants. Remind the designated person that s/he will only have one minute to present.

C. LARGE GROUP PRESENTATIONS

1. Large Group Leader

   Reconvene the Group. Call the small groups back together.

Explain the Procedure. Explain that a representative of each small group will share that group's reflections on applications from the life of Moses with the larger group. Allow time for discussion of "What Do You Think?" questions.

Remind Small Group Representatives of the Time. Remind each small group representative that s/he should try to summarize the group's discussion in one minute. Be sure that the small group presenters connect their summaries to the life of Moses and that they draw parallels between Moses's life and and modern lives among Blacks. By this time, presentations should flow somewhat easily, seeing that most participants will be familiar with the process. However, it may be necessary to pose questions that require them to relate their small group presentations to the chapter's biblical character and generalize it to modern life.

Assignment. Assign participants to read Chapter Six in preparation for the next session.

D. PRAYER

Hold hands, create a circle, and ask for specific prayer requests. Then ask for several volunteers to pray, keeping the prayer requests in mind.

CHAPTER SIX

DEBORAH:
Sister, Take Charge!

Format for Sessions of 90 Minutes or More

PART ONE		PART TWO	
TIME	ACTIVITY	TIME	ACTIVITY
5 min.	Prayer	25 min.	Small Group Study
5 min.	Scripture	20 min.	Large Group Presentations
15 min.	Scripture Search	5 min.	Prayer
15 min.	Chapter Highlights		

For sessions of less than 90 minutes, use PART ONE only, and assign the case study as homework

LESSON AIMS: At the end of this two–part session, participants should be able to: a) describe Deborah's role as ruler and judge; b) explain Deborah's role as prophetess and poet; c) give an example of Deborah's role as agitator; d) describe Deborah's role as wife and mother of Israel; e) apply principles from Deborah's life to lives of African Americans today.

I. PART ONE

A. PRAYER

Open the session with prayer, including the lesson aims.

B. SCRIPTURE

1. Summarize and review Judges 4:1-10, 14-15; 5:1-3
2. Direct their attention to the "Scripture Search" section of the chapter.
3. Ask participants to fill in the blanks with the proper responses.
4. After about ten minutes, ask for volunteers to present their answers.
5. Answers: 1. husband; 2. Jews, Saul; 3. Army; 4. right right, right; 5. ruler, judge, poetess, wife, action.

C. CHAPTER HIGHLIGHTS

Explain that the chapter focuses on Deborah. Use Chapter Six as background, and provide a general overview of the points made in the chapter. Be sure to include the following topics:

1. Deborah: Woman of Many Roles
2. Deborah: Woman of Action
3. Deborah: An Effective Leader

II. PART TWO

A. THE AFRICAN AMERICAN CONNECTION

1. Introduction

   Explain that the "African American Connection" section provides an opportunity to apply principles from Deborah's life to African Americans today.

DEBORAH: SISTER TAKE CHARGE!

2. Procedure

Select Small Group Leaders. Ask for volunteers or select four small group leaders. Then assign each small group leader a number, 1–4. This can be done beforehand. Ask the small group leaders to write their numbers on large sheets of paper so that they can be seen from a distance.

Divide into Small Groups. Inform them that they will form into four small groups. Each group will discuss a different topic, and will then present its findings to the larger group. The topics to be discussed should correspond with the numbers of the groups as follows:

Group #1: Use Our Resources
Group #2: Become Agitators
Group #3: Initiate Liberation
Group #4: Trust God

Allow the Participants to Count Off by Fours. Then ask them to follow the small group leader holding their respective assigned numbers. Inform them of the location where groups will be meeting. These locations can also be printed, beforehand, on a sheet of paper, copied and distributed.

Ask the small group leaders to display their numbers so that persons with that number can follow the leader to the respective meeting places. Then allow them to assemble into the smaller groups.

B. SMALL GROUP STUDY

1. Small Group Leaders

For each topic, there are several related questions designed to stimulate disussion. Therefore, each small group will have one topic to explore.

2. Sharing Insights

After ten minutes, small group leaders should designate someone to summarize the small group discussion within the larger body. Remind the designated person that s/he will only have one minute to present.

C. LARGE GROUP PRESENTATIONS

1. Large Group Leader

Reconvene the Group. Call the small groups back together.

Explain the Procedure. Explain that a representative of each small group will share that group's reflections with the larger group. Allow time for discussion of "What Do You Think?" questions.

Remind Small Group Representatives of the Time. Remind each small group representative that s/he should try to summarize the group's discussion in one minute. Be sure that the small group presenters draw parallels between Deborah's life and modern life. By now most will be familiar with the format, but it may be necessary to pose questions that help them to relate their presentations to Deborah's life and African Americans today.

Assignment. Encourage participants to read Chapter Seven before the next session.

D. PRAYER

Hold hands and, in a circle, ask for specific prayer requests. Then ask for several volunteers to pray, keeping the prayer requests in mind.

CHAPTER SEVEN

SAMUEL:
The Man in the Middle

Format for Sessions of 90 Minutes or More

PART ONE		PART TWO	
TIME	ACTIVITY	TIME	ACTIVITY
5 min.	Prayer	25 min.	Small Group Study
5 min.	Scripture	20 min.	Large Group Presentations
15 min.	Scripture Search	5 min.	Prayer
15 min.	Chapter Highlights		

For sessions of less than 90 minutes, use PART ONE only, and assign the case study as homework

LESSON AIMS: At the end of this two–part session, the participant should be able to: a) present an overview of the birth and childhood of Samuel; b) discuss Samuel's call and preparation for the ministry; c) describe Samuel's accomplishments as a leader over Israel; d) discuss Samuel's relationship with the Lord; e) apply principles from Samuel's life to African Americans today.

ORDINARY PEOPLE CAN DO THE EXTRAORDINARY

I. PART ONE

A. PRAYER

Open the session with prayer, including the lesson aims.

B. SCRIPTURE

1. Summarize and review 1 Samuel 1:9-11, 20, 24-28; 3:1-10.
2. Direct them to the "Scripture Search" section.
3. Ask participants to match the columns.
4. After ten minutes, ask for volunteers to give their answers.
5. Answers: 1. E; 2. D; 3. B; 4. A; 5. C.

C. CHAPTER HIGHLIGHTS

Explain that the chapter focuses on Samuel. Using Chapter Seven as background, provide a general overview of the points made in the chapter. Be sure to include the following:

1. Who Was Samuel?
2. Samuel's Mother, Hannah
3. Samuel's Birth
4. Samuel's Preparation
5. Samuel's Call
6. Samuel's Message
7. Samuel's Sons
8. Samuel and Saul
9. Samuel and David
10. Samuel's Leadership Qualities

II. PART TWO

A. THE AFRICAN AMERICAN CONNECTION

1. Introduction

    Explain that this section provides an opportunity to apply

principles from Samuel's life to African American lives today.

2. Procedure

   Select Small Group Leaders. Ask for volunteers or select three small group leaders. Then assign each small group leader a number, 1–3. This can be done beforehand. Ask the small group leaders to write their numbers on large sheets of paper so that the numbers can be seen from a distance.

   Divide into Small Groups. Inform the participants that they will form three small groups. Each group will discuss a different topic related to Samuel's life, and will present their findings to the larger group at the end of the small group period. The topics to be studied should correspond to the number of groups as follows:

   Group #1 Prayer Is Important
   Group #2 Skill and Character Are Important
   Group #3 Roots Are Important

   Allow the Participants to Count Off by Threes. Ask them to follow the small group leader holding their respective assigned numbers. Inform them of the location where each of the three groups will be meeting. These locations can be printed, beforehand, on paper, copied and distributed.

   Ask the small group leaders to display their numbers so that participants can follow the leaders to their respective meeting places. Allow participants to assemble into smaller groups.

B. SMALL GROUP STUDY

1. Small Group Leaders

   For each topic there are several points of discussion.

Therefore, each small group will have one topic to study.

2. Sharing Insights

After ten minutes, designate someone to summarize the small group discussion within the larger body. Remind the designated person that s/he will only have one minute.

C. LARGE GROUP PRESENTATIONS

1. Large Group Leader

Reconvene the Group. Call the small groups back together.

Explain the Procedure. Explain that a representative of each small group will share that group's reflections with the larger group. Allow time for discussion of "What Do You Think?" questions.

Remind Small Group Representatives of the Time. Remind each small group representative that s/he should try to summarize his/her group's discussion in one minute.

Be sure that the small group presenters connect their small group presentations to the story of Samuel and to modern life. At this point, the group should be familiar with the process. Each small group should focus on a different aspect of the topic, relating it to the Bible.

Assignment. Assign participants to read Chapter eight in preparation for the next session.

D. PRAYER

Hold hands, form a circle, and ask for specific prayer requests. Then ask for several volunteers to pray, keeping the prayer requests in mind.

CHAPTER EIGHT

DAVID:
A Boy from the 'Hood

Format for Sessions of 90 Minutes or More

PART ONE		PART TWO	
TIME	ACTIVITY	TIME	ACTIVITY
5 min.	Prayer	25 min.	Small Group Study
5 min.	Scripture	20 min.	Large Group Presentations
15 min.	Scripture Search	5 min.	Prayer
15 min.	Chapter Highlights		

For sessions of less than 90 minutes, use PART ONE only, and assign the case study as homework

LESSON AIMS: At the end of this two–part session, the participant should be able to: a) present an overview of the life of David; b) identify the many roles that David played in Israel; c) discuss David's achievements; d) describe David's leadership qualities; e) apply principles from David's life to lives of African Americans today.

ORDINARY PEOPLE CAN DO THE EXTRAORDINARY

I. PART ONE

A. PRAYER

Open the session with prayer, including the lesson aims.

B. SCRIPTURE

1. Summarize and review 1 Samuel 16:11-13; 2 Samuel 7:1-3, 14-17.
2. Direct them to the "Scripture Search" section.
3. Instruct students to fill in the blanks to spell out the correct word.
4. After about ten minutes, ask for volunteers to present their answers.
5. Answers: 1. Bethelem; 2. shepherd; 3. Psalms; 4. temple; 5. Solomon.

C. CHAPTER HIGHLIGHTS

Explain that the chapter focuses on David. Using Chapter Eight as background and "Let's Discover" as a starting point, provide a general overview of the points made in the chapter. Be sure to include the following topics:

1. David: Man of Many Roles
2. David: Man of Achievement
3. David: An Effective Leader

II. PART TWO

A. THE AFRICAN AMERICAN CONNECTION

1. Introduction

   Explain that "The African American Connection" provides an opportunity to apply principles from the life of David to modern life.

2. Procedure

Select Small Group Leaders. Ask for volunteers or select three small group leaders. Then assign each small group leader a number, 1–3. This can be done beforehand. Ask the small group leaders to write their numbers on large sheets of paper so that the numbers can be seen from a distance.

Divide into Small Groups. Inform them that they will be forming three small groups. Each group will study a different topic related to David, and will present their findings to the larger group at the end of the small group study period.

As before, the large group leader should vary the composition of small groups. If necessary, explain that it is a good idea to meet and interact with new people. To facilitate this, you will count from a different point in the room than you have previously, thus making it unlikely that anyone will have the same number they had the previous week.

The questions to be discussed should correspond to the number of the group as follows:

Group #1 Talent and Skills
Group #2 Saints and Sinners
Group #3 Love for Our People

Allow the Participants to Count Off by Threes. Then ask them to follow the small group leader holding their respective assigned numbers. Inform them of the location where each of the groups will be meeting.

Ask small group leaders to display their numbers so that people having their numbers can follow them to their respective meeting places. Allow participants to assemble into the smaller groups.

B. SMALL GROUP STUDY

1. Small Group Leaders

   For each topic there are several related questions designed to stimulate discussion within each group.

2. Sharing Insights

   Remind the group leaders that after ten minutes, they should designate someone to summarize the small group discussion for the larger body. The designated person will have a one-minute time limit.

C. LARGE GROUP PRESENTATIONS

1. Large Group Leader

   Reconvene the Group. Call the small groups back together.

   Explain the Procedure. Explain that a representative of each small group will share that group's reflections on applications from David's life.

   Remind Small Group Representatives of the Time. Remind each small group representative to summarize the group's discussion in one minute. Be sure that the small group presenters make connections between Scripture and modern life.

   Assignment. Ask participants to read Chapter Nine before the next session.

D. PRAYER

Hold hands, form a circle, and ask for specific prayer requests. Then ask for several volunteers to pray, keeping the prayer requests in mind.

CHAPTER NINE

SOLOMON:
Lord, Give Me Common Sense

Format for Sessions of 90 Minutes or More

PART ONE		PART TWO	
TIME	ACTIVITY	TIME	ACTIVITY
5 min.	Prayer	25 min.	Small Group Study
5 min.	Scripture	20 min.	Large Group Presentations
15 min.	Scripture Search	5 min.	Prayer
15 min.	Chapter Highlights		

For sessions of less than 90 minutes, use PART ONE only, and assign the case study as homework

LESSON AIMS: At the end of this two–part session, the participant should be able to: a) discuss Solomon's birth and family background; b) present indications from Scripture that Solomon was of African descent; c) identify Solomon's achievements as king of Israel; d) describe Solomon's leadership qualities; e) describe Solomon's final years; f) apply principles from Solomon's life to lives of African Americans.

I. PART ONE

A. PRAYER

Open the session with prayer, including the lesson aims.

B. SCRIPTURE

1. Allow participants to summarize 2 Chronicles 1:1, 6-12; 7:11-18.
2. Direct them to the "Scripture Search" section of the chapter.
3. Ask them to complete the sentences by filling in the blanks with the proper responses.
4. After about ten minutes, ask for volunteers to share their answers.
5. Answers: 1. Bathsheba; 2. wisdom; 3. Queen of Sheba; 4. 700; 5. temple, Jerusalem.

C. CHAPTER HIGHLIGHTS

Explain that the chapter focuses on Solomon. Use Chapter Nine to provide a general overview of the points made in the chapter. Be sure to include the following topics:

1. Solomon's African Heritage
2. Solomon's Ascension to the Throne
3. Solomon's Leadership Characteristics
4. Solomon's Final Years

II. PART TWO

A. THE AFRICAN AMERICAN CONNECTION

1. Introduction

   The "African American Connection" section provides the opportunity to apply principles from Solomon's life to African American lives today.

2. Procedure

Select Small Group Leaders. Ask for volunteers or select three small group leaders. Then assign each small group leader a number, 1–3. This can be done beforehand to facilitate a smoother meeting time. Ask the small group leaders to write their numbers on large sheets of paper so that the numbers can be seen from a distance.

Divide into Small Groups. Inform the participants that they will be forming three small groups. Each group will study a different topic related to the life of Solomon and will present their findings to the larger group at the end of the small group discussion period. The topics should correspond with the number of the group as follows:

Group #1 God's Word: A Source of Insight
Group #2 The Victims: Are They at Fault?
Group #3 Marva Collins: Educational Role Model

Allow the Participants to Count Off by Fives. Ask them to follow the small group leader holding their respective assigned numbers. Inform them of the location where each of the three groups will be meeting. These locations can be printed, beforehand, on a sheet of paper, copied and distributed, so as to facilitate a smoother meeting time.

Ask the small group leaders to display their numbers so that people having their numbers can follow them to their respective meeting places. Then allow the participants to assemble into the smaller groups.

B. SMALL GROUP STUDY

1. Small Group Leaders

For each topic there are several points raised, designed to

stimulate discussion. Therefore, each small group will have one topic to explore.

2. Sharing Insights

Make sure the group leaders know that after ten minutes, they should designate someone to summarize the small group discussion for the larger body of participants. Remind the leaders that the designated person has a one-minute time limit.

C. LARGE GROUP PRESENTATIONS

1. Large Group Leader

Reconvene the Group. Call the small groups back together.

Explain the Procedure. Explain that a representative of each small group will share that group's reflections on applications from the life of Solomon. Allow time for discussion of "What Do You Think?" questions.

Remind Small Group Representatives of the Time. Remind each small group representative to summarize his/her group's discussion in one minute. Be sure that the small group presenters connect their presentations to the chapter's main points.

Assignment. Assign participants to read Chapter Ten between sessions in preparation for the discussion on Elijah at the next session.

D. PRAYER

Hold hands, form a circle, and ask for specific prayer requests. Then ask for several volunteers to pray, keeping the prayer requests in mind.

CHAPTER TEN

ELIJAH:
Strange But Powerful

Format for Sessions of 90 Minutes or More

PART ONE		PART TWO	
TIME	ACTIVITY	TIME	ACTIVITY
5 min.	Prayer	25 min.	Small Group Study
5 min.	Scripture	20 min.	Large Group Presentations
15 min.	Scripture Search	5 min.	Prayer
15 min.	Chapter Highlights		

For sessions of less than 90 minutes, use PART ONE only, and assign the case study as homework

LESSON AIMS: At the end of this two–part session, the participant should be able to: a) present a general overview of Elijah's life; b) describe Elijah's encounters with Ahab and the false prophets; c) describe Elijah's encounter with the widow and her son; d) identify the circumstances surrounding Elijah's departure from this life; e) make applications of principles from Elijah's life to lives of African Americans today.

ORDINARY PEOPLE CAN DO THE EXTRAORDINARY

I. PART ONE

A. PRAYER

Open the session with prayer, including the lesson aims.

B. SCRIPTURE

1. Summarize and review 1 Kings 17:1-6; 18:30-39; 2 Kings 2:11.
2. Direct them to the "Scripture Search" section of the chapter.
3. Ask them to complete the sentences by filling in the blanks.
4. After about ten minutes ask for volunteers to present their answers.
5. Answers: 1. Elijah, Yahweh; 2. Tishbe; 3. Ahab; 4. Carmel; 5. fire.

C. CHAPTER HIGHLIGHTS

Explain that the chapter focuses on Elijah. Using Chapter Ten as background, provide a general overview of the points made. Be sure to include the following topics:

1. Elijah: Last Place in the Fashion Contest
2. Elijah's Life: A Dramatic Series
3. Act 1: The Grand Entrance
a. Act 2: (Scene 1) Elijah and the Widow
b. Act 2: (Scene 2) The Miracle of Life
c. Act 3: (Scene 1) Elijah and Ahab
d. Act 3: (Scene 2) The Great Challenge
e. Act 3: (Scene 3) Enter Jezebel
3. Time Out: Elijah, "Can We Talk?" (1 Kings 19:9-18)
4. Help Wanted: "Where Can I Find a Good Assistant?"
5. Act 4: The Grand Finale

II. PART TWO

A. THE AFRICAN AMERICAN CONNECTION

1. Introduction

   Inform them that this section provides an opportunity to apply principles from Elijah's life to African American lives today.

2. Procedure

   Select Small Group Leaders. Ask for volunteers or select four small group leaders. Try to vary the selection of leaders, so participants each get a chance to lead groups. Then assign each small group leader a number, 1–4. This can be done beforehand. Ask the small group leaders to write their numbers on large sheets of paper so that the numbers can be seen from a distance.

   Divide into Small Groups. Inform them that they will be forming four small groups. Each group will discuss a different topic related to the life of Elijah, and will present its findings to the larger group at the end of the small group discussion. Each topic should correspond to the number of the group as follows:

   Group #1 Is God Interested?
   Group #2 Need A Break?
   Group #3 Who's on the Fence?
   Group #4 Am I Alone?

   Allow the Participants to Count Off by Fours. Then ask them to follow the small group leader holding their respective assigned numbers. Inform them of the location. These locations can be printed, beforehand, on a sheet of paper, copied and distributed. Ask the small group leaders to display their numbers so that people having that number can follow them to the leaders to respective meeting places. Then allow the participants to assemble into the smaller groups.

B. SMALL GROUP STUDY

1. Small Group Leaders

   Each small group will have several related questions on their topic to discuss.

2. Sharing Insights

   After ten minutes, small group leaders should designate someone to summarize the small group discussion within the larger body. The designated person will have only one minute to present.

C. LARGE GROUP PRESENTATIONS

1. Large Group Leader

   Reconvene the Group. Call the small groups back together.

   Explain the Procedure. Explain that a representative of each small group will share that group's reflections on applications from Elijah's life.

   Remind Small Group Representatives of the Time. Remind each small group representative of the one–minute time limit for summarizing his/her group's discussion. Be sure that the small group presenters connect their small group presentations to Scripture and modern life.

   Assignment. Have participants read Chapter Eleven before the next session.

D. PRAYER

Hold hands, form a circle, and ask for specific prayer requests. Then ask for several volunteers to pray, keeping the prayer requests in mind.

CHAPTER ELEVEN

JOSIAH:
It's Not Where You Come From

Format for Sessions of 90 Minutes or More

PART ONE		PART TWO	
TIME	ACTIVITY	TIME	ACTIVITY
5 min.	Prayer	25 min.	Small Group Study
5 min.	Scripture	20 min.	Large Group Presentations
15 min.	Scripture Search	5 min.	Prayer
15 min.	Chapter Highlights		

For sessions of less than 90 minutes, use PART ONE only, and assign the case study as homework

LESSON AIMS: At the end of this two–part session, the participant should be able to: a) present an overview of Josiah's life; b) summarize Josiah's achievements; c) describe Josiah's leadership qualities; d) apply principles from Josiah's life to modern life today.

ORDINARY PEOPLE CAN DO THE EXTRAORDINARY

I. PART ONE

A. PRAYER

Open the session with prayer, including the lesson aims.

B. SCRIPTURE

1. Summarize and review 2 Chronicles 34:1-3, 8, 15, 18-23, 27-28; 25:1, 17, 23-25.
2. Direct participants to the "Scripture Search" section of the chapter.
3. Have participants fill in blanks describing Josiah's work and character.
4. After about ten minutes, ask for volunteers to share their answers.
5. Answers: 1) a-idolatry, b-temple, c-law, d-Passover; 2) a-obedient, b-honest, c-compassionate, d-thorough, e-organized.

C. CHAPTER HIGHLIGHTS

Explain that the chapter focuses on Josiah. Using Chapter Eleven as background and "Let's Discover" as a starting point, provide a general overview of the points made in the chapter. Be sure to include the following topics:

1. Josiah's Achievements
2. Josiah's Leadership Qualities

II. PART TWO

A. THE AFRICAN AMERICAN CONNECTION

1. Introduction

   This section gives participants a chance to apply principles from Josiah's life to African American lives today.

JOSIAH: ITS NOT WHERE YOU COME FROM

2. Procedure

Select Small Group Leaders. Ask for volunteers or select three small group leaders. Then assign each small group leader a number, 1–3. This can be done beforehand. Ask the small group leaders to write their numbers on large sheets of paper so that the numbers can be seen from a distance.

Divide into Small Groups. Inform the participants that they will be forming three small groups. Each group will focus on a different topic related to Josiah's life, and will present its findings to the larger group at the end of the small group discussion.

Each topic should correspond with the number of the group as follows:

Group #1 Handicapped
Group #2 Young, Black and Serious
Group #3 Committed to Change

Allow the Participants to Count Off by Threes. Then ask them to follow the small group leader holding their respective assigned numbers. Inform them of the location of the room (or building) where each of the three groups will be meeting. These locations can be printed, beforehand, on a sheet of paper, copied and distributed, so as to facilitate a smoother meeting time.

Ask the small group leaders to display their numbers so that persons having that number can follow them to their respective meeting places. Then allow the participants to assemble into the smaller groups.

B. SMALL GROUP STUDY

1. Small Group Leaders

   Each small group will have one topic to discuss.

2. Sharing Insights

   After ten minutes, each group leader should designate someone to summarize the small group discussion for the larger body of participants. The designated person will only have one minute to present.

C. LARGE GROUP PRESENTATIONS

1. Large Group Leader

   Reconvene the Group. Call the small groups back together.

   Explain the Procedure. A representative of each small group will share that group's reflections on the life of Josiah. Allow time for discussion of "What Do You Think?" questions.

   Remind Small Group Representatives of the Time. Each small group representative should summarize his/her group's discussion in one minute. Be sure that the small group presenters connect their small group presentations to Scriptures and modern life.

   Assignment. Encourage participants to read Chapter Twelve before the next session.

D. PRAYER

Hold hands, form a circle, and ask for specific prayer requests. Then ask for several volunteers to pray, keeping the prayer requests in mind.

CHAPTER TWELVE

JEREMIAH:
Hope in Spite of Tears

Format for Sessions of 90 Minutes or More

PART ONE		PART TWO	
TIME	ACTIVITY	TIME	ACTIVITY
5 min.	Prayer	25 min.	Small Group Study
5 min.	Scripture	20 min.	Large Group Presentations
15 min.	Scripture Search	5 min.	Prayer
15 min.	Chapter Highlights		

For sessions of less than 90 minutes, use PART ONE only, and assign the case study as homework

LESSON AIMS: At the end of this two–part session, the participant should be able to: a) provide an overview of the life of Jeremiah the prophet; b) describe the historical context in which Jeremiah lived; c) discuss Jeremiah's writings as a poet; d) discuss Jeremiah's ministry; e) discuss Jeremiah's message; f) identify the friends and enemies of Jeremiah; g) draw principles from the life of Jeremiah which apply to African Americans today.

ORDINARY PEOPLE CAN DO THE EXTRAORDINARY

I. PART ONE

A. PRAYER

Open the session with prayer, including the lesson aims.

B. SCRIPTURE

1. Summarize and review Jeremiah 1:1-10; 9:1-2; Lamentations 3:21-26.
2. Direct them to the "Scripture Search" section of the chapter.
3. Ask participants to play "Bible Jeopardy." Instruct students to use each clue to give the proper response in the form of a question.
4. After about ten minutes ask for volunteers to present their answers.
5. Answers: 1. Jeremiah; 2. Anathoth; 3. Lamentations; 4. ministry; 5. message.

C. CHAPTER HIGHLIGHTS

Explain that the chapter focuses on Jeremiah. Use Chapter 12 as background. Then provide a general overview of the points made in the chapter. Be sure to include the following topics:

1. Jeremiah's Roots
2. Jeremiah's Times
3. Jeremiah's Writings
4. Jeremiah's Ministry
5. Jeremiah's Message
6. Jeremiah's Enemies and Problems

II. PART TWO

A. THE AFRICAN AMERICAN CONNECTION

1. Introduction

   This section provides the opportunity to apply principles from Jeremiah's life to African American lives today.

2. Procedure

   Select Small Group Leaders. Ask for volunteers or select three small group leaders. Then assign each small group leader a number, 1–3. This can be done beforehand. Ask the small group leaders to write their numbers on large sheets of white paper so that they can be seen from a distance.

   Divide into Small Groups. Inform the group of participants that they will form three small groups. Each group will discuss a different topic, and will present its findings to the larger group at the end of the small group discussion period. The topics to be discussed should correspond to the number of the group as follows:

   Group #1 Abortion
   Group #2 Leadership
   Group #3 Spiritual Development

   Allow the Participants to Count Off by Threes. Ask them to follow the small group leader holding their respective assigned numbers. Inform them of the location. These locations can also be printed, beforehand, on a sheet of paper, copied and distributed.

   Ask small group leaders to display their numbers so that persons having their number can follow them to meeting places. Allow participants to assemble into the smaller groups.

B. SMALL GROUP STUDY

1. Small Group Leaders

   For each topic, there several related questions designed to stimulate discussion. Therefore, each small group will have one topic to explore.

2. Sharing Insights

   After ten minutes, designate someone to summarize the small group discussion within the larger body of participants. Remind the designated person that she/he will only have one minute to present.

C. LARGE GROUP PRESENTATIONS

1. Large Group Leader

   Reconvene the Group. Call the small groups back together.

   Explain the Procedure. Explain that a representative of each small group will share that group's reflections on Jeremiah's life with the larger group.

   Remind Small Group Representatives of the Time. Remind each small group representative she/he should try to summarize his/her group's discussion in one minute. Be sure that the small group presenters connect their small group presentations to Scripture and modern times.

D. PRAYER

Hold hands, form a circle, and ask for specific prayer requests. Then ask for several volunteers to pray, keeping the prayer requests in mind.